COLOUR IN
FRENCH

Catherine Bruzzone
Illustrations: Clare Beaton
French: Claudine Bharadia

b small publishing

1 **le soleil**
sun

2 **les vagues**
waves

3 **le voilier**
sailing boat

4 **la balle**
ball

5 **le chapeau de paille**
sun hat

6 **les lunettes de soleil**
sunglasses

7 **la glace**
ice-cream

8 **le maillot de bain**
swimming costume

9 **la serviette**
towel

10 **le parasol**
beach umbrella

À la plage
At the beach

11 le poisson
fish

12 la mouette
seagull

13 le rocher
rock

14 le véliplanchiste
windsurfer

15 la mer
sea

16 le requin
shark

17 le sable
sand

18 le seau
bucket

19 la pelle
spade

20 le château de sable
sandcastle

21 le coquillage
shell

1 l'immeuble
block of flats

2 le train
train

3 le supermarché
supermarket

7 le parking
car park

8 le restaurant
restaurant

9 le magasin
shop

13 le camion
lorry

14 la voiture
car

15 le vélo
bicycle

4 la gare
railway station

5 le parc
park

6 l'école
school

10 la station-service
petrol station

11 le bus
bus

12 l'arrêt de bus
bus stop

En ville
In town

16 la maison
house

17 le trottoir
pavement

18 la rue
road

1 **les décorations**
decorations

2 **le ballon**
balloon

3 **le masque**
mask

4 **le gâteau**
cake

5 **les bougies**
candles

6 **la boisson**
drink

7 **la paille**
straw

8 **le verre**
glass

9 **la carafe**
jug

C'est la fête!
Let's celebrate!

10 le chapeau en papier
party hat

11 le cadeau
present

12 la tasse
cup

13 la carte
card

14 les bonbons
sweets

15 les chips
crisps

16 l'assiette
plate

17 les mini-cakes
buns

Les couleurs
Colours

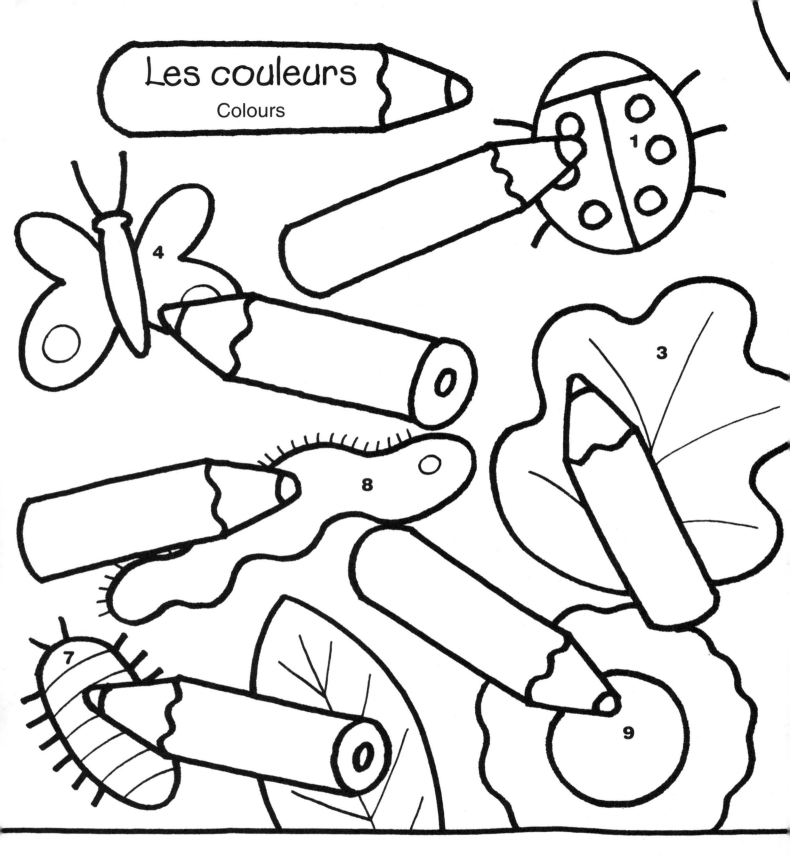

1 rouge red	**2** jaune yellow	**3** vert green
7 gris grey	**8** marron brown	**9** orange orange

4 bleu
blue

5 noir
black

6 blanc
white

10 rose
pink

11 violet
purple

1 la tête
head

2 les cheveux
hair

3 l'œil
eye

4 le nez
nose

5 l'oreille
ear

6 la bouche
mouth

7 le cou
neck

8 l'épaule
shoulder

9 le bras
arm

10 la main
hand

11 la jambe
leg

12 le pied
foot

Le corps
The body

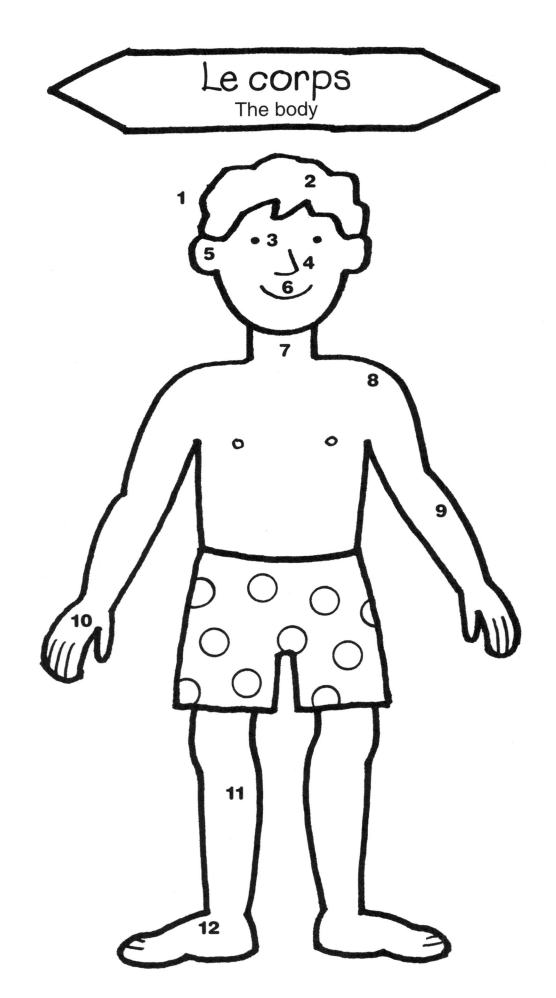

1 le chapeau
hat

2 l'écharpe
scarf

3 le pull
jumper

4 la jupe
skirt

5 les chaussettes
socks

6 les chaussures
shoes

7 la chemise
shirt

8 le pantalon
trousers

9 les chaussons
slippers

10 la robe
dress

11 le short
shorts

12 le pyjama
pyjamas

Mes vêtements
My clothes

1 la chambre
bedroom

2 le lit
bed

3 la commode
chest of drawers

7 la fenêtre
window

8 le tableau
picture

9 la lumière
light

Ma maison My house

13 le salon
sitting room

14 le fauteuil
armchair

15 la lampe
lamp

19 la télévision
television

20 l'horloge
clock

21 la porte
door

4 la salle de bains
bathroom

5 la baignoire
bath

6 la douche
shower

10 le miroir
mirror

11 le lavabo
washbasin

12 les cabinets
toilet

16 la cuisine
kitchen

17 la cuisinière
cooker

18 l'évier
sink

22 la chaise
chair

23 la table
table

24 le frigo
fridge

Au marché

At the market

Les fruits

Fruit

les cerises
cherries

les melons
melons

les prunes
plums

les poires
pears

les pommes
apples

les fraises
strawberries

l'ananas
pineapple

les raisins
grapes

les oranges
oranges

les bananes
bananas

les citrons
lemons

Les légumes
Vegetables

les carottes
carrots

les pommes de terre
potatoes

les tomates
tomatoes

les haricots
beans

la laitue
lettuce

les champignons
mushrooms

le céleri
celery

l'ail
garlic

les oignons
onions

1 le poisson
fish

2 la viande
meat

3 le caddie
shopping trolley

7 le pain
bread

8 le dentifrice
toothpaste

9 le yaourt
yoghurt

Au supermarché
At the supermarket

13 l'huile
oil

14 le beurre
butter

15 la confiture
jam

18 les pâtes
pasta

19 le sucre
sugar

20 le shampooing
shampoo

4 les boîtes de conserve
tins

5 les œufs
eggs

6 la farine
flour

10 le chocolat
chocolate

11 les gâteaux secs
biscuits

12 le lait
milk

16 le savon
soap

17 la bouteille
bottle

21 le fromage
cheese

22 le sac
bag

Temps libre!
Time off!

regarder la télévision
watching television

jouer au football
playing football

lire
reading

jouer au basket-ball
playing basketball

faire du vélo
cycling

nager
swimming

faire du skateboard
skateboarding

danser
dancing

1 Il y a des nuages
It's cloudy

2 l'arc-en-ciel
rainbow

3 Il y a du soleil
It's sunny

4 Il fait chaud
It's hot

5 le tonnerre
thunder

6 l'éclair
lightning

7 l'orage
storm

8 Il pleut
It's raining

Le temps et les saisons
Weather and seasons

Le printemps — Spring

L'été — Summer

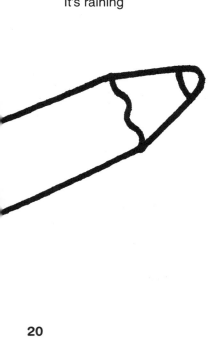

L'automne — Autumn

L'hiver — Winter

9

10

11

12

9 Il y a du vent
It's windy

10 Il y a du brouillard
It's foggy

11 Il neige
It's snowing

12 Il fait froid
It's cold

1 le père/papa
father/dad

2 la mère/maman
mother/mum

3 le grand-père/pépé
grandfather/grandpa

7 le bébé
baby

Ma famille
My family

11 la tante
aunt

12 la fille
daughter

13 le fils
son

4 la grand-mère/mémé
grandmother/granny

5 l'oncle
uncle

6 le mari
husband

8 la femme
wife

9 le garçon
boy

10 la fille
girl

14 le frère
brother

15 la sœur
sister

16 les jumeaux
twins

1 la cour
playground

2 l'ordinateur
computer

3 l'imprimante
printer

4 le papier
paper

5 l'écolière
girl pupil

6 le bureau
desk

7 le stylo
pen

8 la gomme
rubber

9 la règle
ruler

10 le cahier
exercise book

À l'école
At school

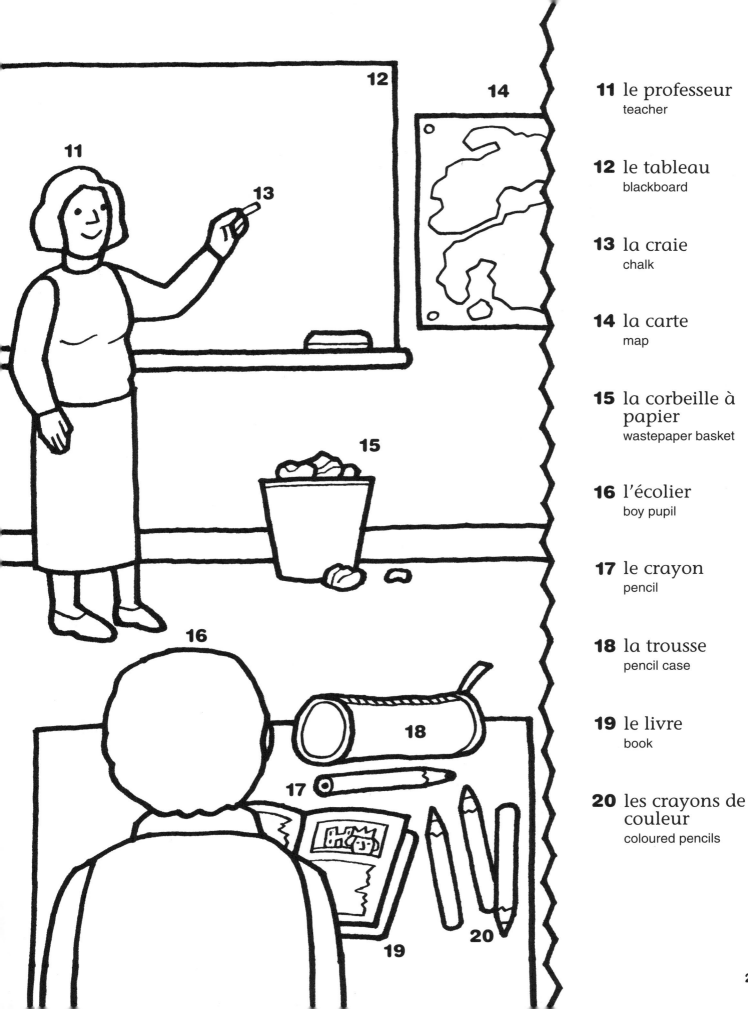

11 le professeur
teacher

12 le tableau
blackboard

13 la craie
chalk

14 la carte
map

15 la corbeille à papier
wastepaper basket

16 l'écolier
boy pupil

17 le crayon
pencil

18 la trousse
pencil case

19 le livre
book

20 les crayons de couleur
coloured pencils

1 la montagne
mountain

2 la forêt
forest

5 le champ
field

6 le buisson
bush

À la campagne
In the countryside

9 la rivière
river

10 le pont
bridge

13 la fleur
flower

14 le papillon
butterfly

3 l'arbre
tree

4 la feuille
leaf

7 le chemin
path

8 la clôture
fence

11 la barrière
gate

12 l'oiseau
bird

15 le lac
lake

16 la grenouille
frog

À la ferme
On the farm

1 **le tracteur**
tractor

2 **le fermier**
farmer

3 **le mouton**
sheep

4 **le cochon**
pig

5 **le chat**
cat

6 **le chien**
dog

7 **la souris**
mouse

8 la grange
barn

9 la vache
cow

10 le cheval
horse

11 le coq
cock

12 la chèvre
goat

13 la poule
hen

14 l'oie
goose

15 le canard
duck

1 le lion
lion

2 le tigre
tiger

5 l'ours
bear

6 le rhinocéros
rhinoceros

9 l'éléphant
elephant

10 le gardien de zoo
zoo keeper

13 le kangourou
kangaroo

14 le pingouin
penguin